The Impossible
Dream

The Impossible Dream

Jean Parkin

Copyright © Jean Parkin.

All rights reserved. No part of this book may be reproduced in any form or by any electronic or mechanical means, including information storage and retrieval systems, without permission in writing from the publisher, except by reviewers, who may quote brief passages in a review.

ISBN: 978-1-63649-261-2   (Paperback Edition)
ISBN: 978-1-63649-262-9   (Hardcover Edition)
ISBN: 978-1-63649-260-5   (E-book Edition)

Book Ordering Information

Phone Number: 315 288-7939 ext. 1000 or 347-901-4920
Email: info@globalsummithouse.com
Global Summit House
www.globalsummithouse.com

Printed in the United States of America

CONTENTS

Introduction ix
Dedication xi

Part 1: Poem; The Elderly 1
Part 2: Redemption in Aging 17

Synopsis 29
Bio 31

INTRODUCTION

Many changes have occurred in life in the process of aging, but none has become as stationary and blocked as those that is the way people age today. The elderly is caught in a swirl of social changes that has left them far behind, even totally out of society. They have become the walking dead, unable to be stirred to enthusiasm, embracing the most morbid depths of their soul. Like the created creature of Frankenstein, society has created the contorted life of the elderly in modern times, whereby the elderly had been robbed of the natural freedoms of the last years of life, before reaching their full humanity as a natural course of daily living, overflowing with promise and hope. Instead of experiencing the grandest of expectations, it has been turned into barren lifeless years.

It is about the aging of healthy individuals, whom suddenly, after retirement, are confronted with walls of discrimination of orwellian nature, laying the foundations of neurosis and inferiority in most every one. This change is not without dire consequences, mostly of inferior quality and a feeling of redundancy as human beings. Some of these problems are discussed in a thoughtful way, with suggestions of eliminating the ugliness and distaste of aging in modern times. It is not a critique of the very old, or the very ill, rather intended for those in the process of becoming elderly. It is not a project of research or statistics, merely an observation of life around us. Life in the Malls, streets, Churches, ordinary people in ordinary circumstances. Specialists in the Medical field have not been consulted, nor has the opinions of elderly people sought. It is just about the elderly in their daily existence, choking on loneliness and neglect.

DEDICATION

For my lovely family of five, Norman, Ingrid, {Renier}, Andrew,{Jayne},Sonya and Donald.
For my ten grandchildren.

For my brother Koos Bothma, Wildlife Ecologist and international author.

Posthumusly, for my husband, Don

PART ONE

Poem; The Elderly

Old
a word for the ugly,
descriptive of decrepitude,
regressive,
devoid of life or
the promise there of,
feared
by most, hopeful of avoiding,
the breaking down,
the pity and
loathing,

its association with death,
Yearning
for the blessings of
sleep,
yet insomnia is all there is.
Or,
the eternal exhaustion of
boredom,
in a world gone dull.
The soul,
abandoned by man and God
shrieks and shrieks,
It can tell of many things,
labels, names, tags,
as if at an auction.
Their voices are faint,
have no audience,
Some opt for
euthanasia,
cannot tell of
the wrath of God,
the lonely world of regret,
but do tell of the
forsaken Doctor,
fraudulent to himself,
traitorous
to honour and duty,
the pledge of healing.
Hurried into oblivion,

The Impossible Dream

faking interest and kindness.
Denied the joy of progress,

Excellence
viewed with amusement,
a relic of the past.

Abilities
decline with lack of
encouragement
or recognition.
Floundering mentally with no
direction,
vocabulary lost in
loneliness, the only
companion.
Grouped together is not the answer,
constrained as humans,
empty hearts filled with longing,
not for youth,
but intellectual satisfaction
in word and deed.   Jean Parkin.

Generous God, you have reached into the lives of Abraham and Sarah, and asked them to dream the impossible dream. Like them, may we believe that you can transform what appears barren and lifeless into a situation overflowing with promise and hope.
(Source of quote unknown)

Our attitude and acceptance of aging, has been transmitted through centuries

of unquestioning acceptance and forbearance, compliance and even indifference.

Changes in science, philosophy, expectation, ambition, have been slow to reach

populations, rural or otherwise. People were contented, stimulation was never sought.

This vacuum, was solidly defended by convention. Change of lifestyle was suspect.

Ideas and habits were entrenched.

Modern influences have uprooted many of the old beliefs. Instead of life becoming

simpler, it has become more complicated. The gap between the younger generation

and the older has widened because of the early maturation of children today and

their demand for the spoils of life at a much younger age as before. In opposition

to this is the stagnation of the older generation. Generations are not in lockstep

anymore. There are significant signs of contempt for each from both sides.

Stagnation is the prime killer of enterprise, higher thinking and achievement.

Viewing this point in all honesty, one has to concede its validity. Nothing of

interest emerges from the elderly. They look alike, think alike, do alike.

This vulnerability comes as a deep shock. Grey hair, wrinkles, sagging skin,
    large all around, shuffling instead of walking, too many changes to count.
    The terrible shock of

        the breaking down,
        the pity or
        loathing,
        its association with death.

    The breaking down!
    Loss of teeth, sight, hearing, walking, working, too many to name! Overcome with
    feelings of deep pain, and in mourning for the self, the loss of beauty,
    health, their place in society.
    Everybody tries to move away from the reality that is the mirror, or the shop
    window. In their self loathing an understanding is born of why young people
    avoid them. The truth is that the elderly are ugly in a world that dotes on beauty,
    freshness and sparkling personalities.
    The new image is too raw, too strong to accommodate comfortably, too uncomfortable
    to bear the sight of.

>   Yearning
>   for the blessing
>   of sleep,
>   yet insomnia
>   is all there is

Their peers are unable to offer sympathy, for they are mirror images of each
    other. Sore hearts and bruised egos are consoled with too much food, wine,
    or beer. Bellies portrude like massive tables below ribcages, or a huge behind,
    often covered in bright colours.
    Symmetry and beauty is lost forever. Some become so grossly fat, that families
    have to be pitied. How Doctors manage an examination boggles the mind.

>   or the eternal
>   exhaustion
>   of boredom,
>   in a world gone
>   dull.

BOREDOM!

The agony of long, lonely days ravaged by boredom. Sleepless nights
    added to the mix. How do they stay sane?

Aging does not wrinkle the spirit, or freeze the mind. No, it only disintegrates
 the place they fill in the world, makes them live in places without centres,
 places where there is no permanence, except the permanence of unwelcome.

 Abandoned by man and God,
  they shriek and shriek.

 There never was any training, a manual to refer to when overwhelmed, traumatized,
 lost in a desert of new sensations, new rules, nobody of elder experience
 to turn to. They are the elderly. Without experience!
 They want to shout it out to the world, they dont want the false teeth, ever
 stronger glasses, walkers, hearing aides!They want to look and feel good!Present
 themselves as intelligent, smart!They dont want to be pitied, grabbed by the arms
 to steady their feet. Feet shod in the flattest most unattractive shoes around.
 They want to tell of the times when they wore heels, walking like camels, even
 stooping in the effort to stay upright. And mostly, they want to tell of their
 loss of dignity, their battles to adapt!
 At certain times we all have to rise above ourselves in order to change, improve or end certain features of living

that are not beneficial anymore. This is particularly true when we reach the uncertain stage of Snr. Citizenship. Aging is an ugly process, and not aided by adding tags to it which are mostly unflattering and unkind. They are treated like potential simpletons, aided by children who have taken over their decisions and actions, yes and no's, aims and hope, even the clothes they shall wear. In fact, they are solely responsible for all their woes, subjugation, tyrants and ever lowering rank. They need to look at themselves with the eyes of those around them, especially younger ones. They also need to be quite honest in their observations, and call themselves out for the needed change and respect to be reinstated.

The times coming are not easy, the loneliness devastating, the fear of aging overwhelming. When getting up in the morning, the inactivity of the coming day lies like a thick blanket over the day. How to fill the day meaningfully, where to go, what to do just to be productive while you can? Whom to love and care for, to have a little conversation with? Many questions remain unanswered. There are no scripts with instructions for managing aging.

The elderly is a large percentage of the population, and collectively a wide source of thought, new ideas. There will be answers but where to start?

>
> They can tell of many
> things,
> labels, tags, references,
> their voices are faint,
> have no audience,

opt for euthansia,
unable to tell of the
wrath of God.

A good place would be the pain and devastation of loneliness from which thousands suffer. Is there help anywhere for this misery? Many opt for the scandalous option of euthanasia, a blot on the laws of a country! So easy! Just pass a law! Parlaiment is supreme! God does not count! Who cares anyway? There are so many of them, commodities cost money. Who cares about the lost soul, the Holy Spirit, Gift of all gifts?

The simple minded wont ask any questions, the intelligent have rejected it long
    ago. Who has returned to tell if the spirit is in peace, or drifting over spheres
    unknown to man? Where is the Pastor, servant to God?
    The conscience of the Holy Church sullied! Bullied by the bullies of law, of the State.

In the lonely world of regret,
The forsaken Doctor,
traitorous
to honour and duty,
the pledge of healing.
Hurried into oblivion,
denied the joy of progress,
For they are old.

Two things should always be considered, management and love. How best to manage life?

The Spirit of God lives in humanity, given to the new born baby in breath, the sacred gift of life. Whatever happens, however and whichever way life goes, the gift of life is always there. It can become a life of great things, a life worth living, leaving a legacy of hope at the end.

It is an elevating thought, to aspire to, an ideal held sacred. The physical body in accordance with thoughtful desire and care, can be taken care of. It will be denied the ravages of smoking, drinking in excess, drugs, abuse of any kind. That in turn will preserve health and a strong mind.

In offering, or demanding euthanasia, to escape pain, loneliness, disillusionment, is a crushing defeat of and to the spirit. Those who arrive at that point, need greater personal care of both body and mind. It should be part of assisted care programs at hospitals to encourage patients to such aid, instead of pushing them to the edge of darkness with assisted suicide. It is essential to the mental health of all to feel useful.

Unhappily, families fail to help their aged to live useful positive lives, by

The Impossible Dream

locking them into dwellings, or rooms, where they rot away in misery and loneliness.

A recurring thought often is "how do I organise my life?" What is a grand idea,

and how to go after it?" Anything rather than the void of elderly living, the

disaster of nothing.

To observe the world of the elderly, sit in a Doctor's waiting room for an hour.

They come in their numbers, huge men, stooped, ravaged by age, men who had given

their powers to their careers, families and country. They are in the night of

existence, standing finger alone against a world of vagary, while experiencing

the soul destroying effects of the vanishing world of the self, the breaking

down of the spirit.

Is it too much to hope for deliverance, the easing of pain? Since it is not

relevant to the present generation alone, improvements will benefit all.

excellence viewed with
amusement.
a relic

of the past,
abilities decline,

recognition and encouragement.
support withheld.

Is there help anywhere from this bondage? Where to find it? How to impose it? The elderly as so many individuals should amalgate into one entity as a Group, or Club or Society. As such, they should acquire status, respected as such in a lawful manner and operate as other groups do. This way many odious manners will disappear and many rights to life restored. One of the first comes to mind. The right to pleasure in all its purity and sweetness, in whichever form it is sought. That includes open freedoms to start up conversations without fear of misconceptions, risking taunts and unsavoury speculation. There is the right to frivolity and opinion. More often than not, the elderly are too timid to give an opinion in conversation, as discrimination can be cold and deadly. The pleasure of affection, the giving and taking of love, the pleasure of lifting the human heart high in expectation of happiness, worth and joy. Sadly for many companionship, human connection and recourse is shadowed by the silence of loneliness. Not only shadowed but wiped out by the pain and abandonment of loneliness. What everyone hopes for at the end of life is seeking contentment, and happiness,.

Aging is a brutal condition, cruel and ugly. How do they stay relevant without falling into this appalling state of existence? What does it take before society starts thinking on the hard question of the last years?Everybody has a right to happiness for life, and to do what gives pleasure. Authorities, local and Governmental usurp that right in many dictatorial ways, to an extent that leave the elderly frightened and insecure. There is fire and tragedy in youth, acceptance and shame in old age. It has become a pattern of cynical aversion.

Young people have claimed for themselves the fashion of familiarity. Gone are the days when a prefix was used in addressing someone older than yourself. It has created a level of familiarity equal to disrespect and disdain. We all know the saying of familiarity breeds contempt.

Many of the elderly are responsible for their own degeneration of the mind through excessively long times sitting watching television, and doing nothing else, creating a lazy mind that does not react to stimuli of reading, debating and free conversation, higher thought being absent from daily intercourse.

    Those things contribute to the early
    demise of a healthy mind. For good vocabulary, one has to use words to remember,
    and to form opinions and ideas.
    One of the elderly problems is that they become one of the herd in society, one
    on the fringe. Those who try to remain individuals are ignored, and become one
    of the avoided, too pitiful to be of importance, a human pile, without dignity
    or rights.
    They dont understand the digital world, the names and function of icons. Their
    world has changed and their place in it is lost. Are they defeated? Why, yes of course!

How does it show? It shows in their diminished sense of being. It shows in their
    humble acceptance of a fake life, in bad unattractive clothing, personal grooming
        and non interest in provoking thought or discourse. Their lives have become cheap
        in a cheap society.
        Yet is is also true the human spirit needs companionship, the warmth of friendship
        to thrive. Feelings of inadequacy and impotance can be overwhelming, affecting
        the most natural desires, to the point of abolishment.

        Floundering mentally,
        with no direction,
        shame filled,
        vocabulary short,
        loneliness
        the only companion,
        constrained,
        grouped,
        a poor answer to
        talent.

    Being alive costs much. It demands hard continuous work, dedication, faith and
        much more. It demands respect, gratitude, generosity and love. It demands idealism,
        anarchy at the right time, to break the hard and fast rules laid down by centuries

The Impossible Dream

of sameness. It demands the fire of new thoughts, new approaches, new rules, new

hope to flourish, but to still live morally imbued. The herd generates a floundering

mentality, unable to establish permanence, drifting into uncertainty. Resources

have shrunk, not by design, but by modern standards. They dont dream anymore. Negative

notions are hard to bear, having, given up on themselves.

People who dont dream anymore infect the world with darkness. The elderly have been

conditioned by generations of predecessors as being useless, disabled by discrimination

to the right to live fully and happily.

Even today, with al the expert information and all kinds of expertise, it is still

about accepting the unacceptable, and not about clearing the way for mind and spirit

to the well-being of uncluttered free thought and spirit.

empty hearts,
filled with longing,
not for youth,
but acceptance and
intellectual satisfaction
and love.   J. Parkin 2009.

PART 2

Redemption in Aging

The elderly will find refuge
and restoration, where
deep within the soul
the Spirit
dwells in union
with man,
helping, encouraging, lending
the weight of
redemption,
strenghthening, faith,
love,

Jean Parkin

and liberty.
They shall find the nerve
for resistance,
the flesh and blood
to overcome.
The precious seed of life
for all their days,
not just some.

To cement their fancies,
and joyfully live.
The blemished heart
will overthrow
indignity,
tyranny,
the lacerations of loneliness.
Heads of white will be as
a wig,
the furrowed brow
as a mask,
the pain of infirmity lessened
by a touch
a kiss,
the care of concern.
The frozen mien,
hiding fear,
will break,
anticipation a sun of pleasure.
Thus in trust
friendship and confidence

The Impossible Dream

>   the hand of premature death
>   might be broken,
>   the full light of life
>   restored.   Jean Parkin 2009.

   The Spirit makes us holy in life, bold in witness, humble in service, and strong
        in hope.   Rev. Fraser Coltman.

>   Let the sweet waters
>   of the heart
>   rise and overflow,
>   Let the tinselled sun
>   drape itself on
>   verdant bough,
>   dispatch pressing thought,
>   Let life abound.   Jean Parkin.

REDEMPTION!

   A friend had recently undergone certain medical tests at the Hospital, and came away very amused. " The nurse treated me like a little old lady" she laughed. Why treat elderly women like little old ladies? A good question. Dare one say, because it is the norm, society's idea of treating elderly people. Patronise them! That is the only way. Which is at best, disrespectful and insulting. What is wrong with professional manners when treating elderly patients?

Overhearing a conversation in a Doctor's waiting room starting with the word "in aging". Why so much punch on aging? What is wrong with the word "living?" Why does everybody forget that the elderly are very much alive, sensitive, and very vulnerable because of the enduring discrimination they face? Why is age and old such a part of people's thoughts? What is wrong with remembering good times, life, happiness, and the many benefits from it? There is so much to be thankful for, so much that delights and pleases. When life is nothing more than ordinary, it is corrupted.

Do not doubt how precious each life is, especially in the face of derision, abuse, loneliness, restrictions and regrets. To be cut off from the living is death! To sit in a chair all day is death! Life is vigour, plans, dreams, activity, creative and enjoyable. Why is it that it is always expected of the elderly to be self sacrificing? To endure the bitter loss of human conversation, stay home, or to gather in a contrived crowd of strangers for amusement? Why do they accept these draconian measures? Why cant they demand better?

Firstly, defy the rules, cut loose the ropes that bind, shake off the weight of oppression. How? Simply dont bandy about your age as if it is something sacred. It is not.

Life is vigour, plans! It is so easy to despair, to look around and just see the
ugliness. It is still a beautiful world, graciously, sublimely created, with people
in it with heart and love, followers of Christ's gentle directions. Though there is

a bite to the years like a stone in the mouth. Ways must be found to diminish
its misery, ways to uphold the adage of being your own master.
Rebellion is a strong bold reaction to inner defeatism so destructive to body and
soul. How to rebel? Defy archaical rules of aging!
By upholding the passage of time as a reason for existence, the deepest reason for
existence is aborted, which is to be of service to our fellowman, upholding God's
commandment of love and purpose.
Obsession with age is also one of the reasons the young shun the elderly. The elderly's fear and hopelessness generates its own retardation.

Strenghthening faith, love
and liberty,
they shall find the nerve
for resistance,
the flesh and blood to overcome.
the precious seeds of life
for all their days,
not just some.

There is a lot to be said for personal grooming. Some give the impression that presenting themselves as attractively as possible is of no importance anymore. Women with long grey hair, no style other than hanging straight down to the shoulders, are a sight for sore eyes. Older women just dont look their best with locks hanging straight down, when styles of coif are versatile and attractive. Granted, lack of finances are a factor, but surely not in every case. There are many options for older women, money saving options with reduced charges. Why does every head have to be snow white when there are other choices?

Do the eyebrows just have to be an invisible line above the eyes? They are the focus of the face and using a dark eyebrow pencil to accentuate the brow curve would be startling and look so good. An eyebrow pencil is affordable and longlasting, and needs only oneself for application. The result would change a grey face into a vivid picture. A little mascara on the lashes will be miraculous. Beauties of former times will be resurrected again by pampering their eyes. Imagine how exciting elderly faces will be, a joy to ponder their hidden beauties!

The lips! Those dry, grey, colourless fossils over the mouth! What is wrong with a peachy or rose coloured lipstick? Those same bloodless lips must have been flashy and red in younger years! Why go totally bare when a little colour really matters and will gave the face quite another expression, one of whimsy, interest, life.

The crinkled skin is not a problem if the other features can be brightened. A wel cared skin with a little foundation will bring the beauty of any woman to the fore again, and will be quite delightful to see. Life is filled with delight, become part of it, not just a bystander looking in from outside.

Lets also discuss the importance of dress. Why not dress to flatter? Why be a size XXL when XL ot just L will be so much more attractive and easily attainable. Bring down the oversized derriere, bosom, arms and calves, the enormous stomach. It can be done slowly but surely by the regular exercise of walking, and complementing that, cutting down on the amount of food eaten., especially starches and sugars. It is such fun to see the difference taking place, and enjoying the power of self discipline, not to forget the improvement in health.

How exciting to go shopping for a new YOU. How encouraging to hear hearty compliments!

But what is good for the goose is also good for the gander. Men are physically and hormonally advantaged, also need overhauling. Two things come to mind instantly. the flowing white beard and the disgusting barrel of a stomach. Imagine not being able to tie your shoe laces, the stomach is in the way. Must there be a beard? Unless you want to look ancient, get rid of it. Why cover a handsome face with white hair?

>The precious seeds of life
>for all their days,
>not just some.
>To end the grip of the haughty,
>to cement their fancies
>and joyfullty live.

Lean upon each other, not in fateful discouragement, but in hopeful encouragement. To
joyfully live! How intoxicating that sounds! As indeed loneliness and boredom

are two great factors preventing joyful living in the life of the elderly. Another
problem for pressure is a shortage of income. There is a perception that the fixed
income of a pension never needs adjustment, though the cost of living affects all
in the same way. It is heartbreaking to see the elderly bag cuts of inferior meat
because it is affordable. Summer fruit, some slyly packed to hide mold, second day old
bread, vegetables that are limp with age, all reasons for rising anxiety when inflation
is out of control.

The blemished heart
will overthrow
indignity,
tyranny,
the laceration of
loneliness.

The elderly need to move forward more aggressively, developing their inner depths,
which can only happen when remaining in the world, and not withdrawing from it.
The world is where the living are, where the sun shines, children laugh and play.
These depths are still valid, God given, meant as guides to the individual.

The Impossible Dream

    How to do it? Soaring in thought and deed, in faith of what is right
    and righteous, in hope for change, intellectualy alive and interesting, stimulating
    and stimulated.
    Away with the selfinflicted burdens of dejection, loss of selfworth, despair! Energise
    painful joints and muscles with slow deliberate exercise, diminish prescriptions,
    participate, create, achieve!
    Play your instruments, practice, pick up your sewing, painting, sculpting, writing
    Exercise the flat voice, it will ring and be beautiful again and believe, believe, believe!
    The careless discarding of identity on the premise of aging is ridiculous and un-
    acceptable. Society is the poorer for it. There is only one way of brightening
    the dim eye of aging, and that is by contemplative thought of revival.

Heads of white
will be as a wig,
the furrowed brow a mask,
The pain of infirmity lessened
by a touch,
a kiss,
the care of concern.

W. B. Yeats began a poem on being old, by saying;" When you are old and gray and full

of sleep".How about waking up, the sun might or might not shine, the soul is alive,

waiting to come to full life again. Wake up!For those empty moments when rising in the

morning, have a goal. Carpe Diem! The day is waiting!

Bring back the flame of life, it is still burning!It has a function for all time!It

lights the way when life is hard, severe.

It is not their youth the elderly need, but its joy, its direction, its affirmation.

The best in man's character, its strenghts, should not be abandoned when low, but

summoned to raise the spirit when needed, connect with the fabric of life.

Do not have expectations, not from family, children, friends, only from yourself.

Self improvement is a self applied job. Apply it with faith and diligence. Dont open

it to discussion. Negative comments abound and are destructive.

The chains of elder discrimination, abuse, rejection, are yours to break, and it will

be tough. It can be done.

The successful will feel the new glow of real life once again, the spark lighting

the mind, replacing ennui with energy, ambition, desire. It will be the pilot flame of

The Impossible Dream

better health, vitality, interest in higher thinking and searching. Better health

is of the essence. Regular walking, light stretching, eating moderately, will

encourage mobility, revitalising body and mind. New energy will create interest in

new goals, lustre in forgotten endeavours. The frame of the body will become upright.

secure and proud. There will be a return to excitement in conversation, deflect

thoughts from pervasive feelings of depression and loneliness.

It will be like living in a new world, walkers put aside, shoulders straight, pain

alleviated by happiness and wellbeing.

> The frozen mien hiding fear
> will break,
> anticipation a sun of pleasure.
> Thus in trust,
> friendship and confidence,
> the hand of premature death,
> might be stayed,
> the full light of life
> restored!

What a wonderful legacy to leave to the young. Dream that impossible dream, live

life out, lessen regrets, achieve spiritual fulfillment, the compass on life's way.

Jean Parkin

    Be a new generation of liveliness, demand courtesy and respect as humans. It is
    a basic need to have access to life and the living! God grant the impossible Dream!

    The END.

SYNOPSIS

The Impossible Dream is about changing the disillussionment and mental ravages of aging into a time of new goals, vigour, happiness and joy, by following a few different strategies, conserving health and wellbeing.

BIO

She qualified as a Medical Tecnologist in Histology and Cytology. She is a trained Soprano and Recitalist. She was married to the late Dr. Don Parkin and has five children. She loves the power and beauty of the written word and human endeavour excites her. She has written three books, two of poetry and one on a life of a family's struggles and sacrifices in her husband's quest to become a Physician. She believes in Sir Ernest Shackleton's motto, " by endurance we conquer". She lives on Vancouver Island with her family.

Books.
GARDEN GOSSIP....2009.
GARDEN TALK......2014
"Is HE a DOCTOR?" 2016.

www.ingramcontent.com/pod-product-compliance
Lightning Source LLC
LaVergne TN
LVHW091935070526
838200LV00068B/1243